CINEMA VERNACULAR
Peter Nickowitz

isbn: 978 1 62462 076 8

Published by
Publication Studio
717 SW Ankney Street
Portland, Oregon 97205
www.publicationstudio.biz

CINEMA VERNACULAR

poems

Peter Nickowitz

For my father, Arlen

TABLE OF CONTENTS

I.

II.

III.

I.

THESE MONTHS
Part One: May

INT. MANHATTAN APARTMENT—TWILIGHT

The walls are thin and the neighborhood bustles,

dull roar

traffic streams through
the window

like smoke from a nearby chimney.
This is the time of day when light is orange & smells
yeast and sesame.
Everything outside imposes

onto a blank room & fills it,
the furniture of an empty one-bedroom.

The cinema knows too much
Its love scenes precede mine.

EXT. WASHINGTON SQUARE SIDEWALK—SAME

A solitary MAN, a crowded street

He is: NICHOLAS BARR, 32, tall & lean,
thoughtful, disheveled,

kicks an empty
Campbell's soup can.

CLOSE UP on Nicholas's foot, CLOSE UP on soup can.
Can against foot feels like nothing, like absence.

The world is crepuscular,
by this light everything is made to curve.

The air tastes of rain but our *hero,*

empty-handed,
won't scare.

EXT. WASHINGTON SQUARE BROWNSTONE—DAY

Nicholas stops before a brownstone.
Checks his watch, the façade beckons: hurry up.

Leaves along the sidewalk,
gather and stir, whirling, like water going down a drain.

INT. PSYCHOANALYST'S OFFICE—DAY

On a daybed covered in red
Nicholas lies,

surrounded by pillows, behind
an analyst sits at a round, pedestal table,
she is ISABEL, late-40s, auburn-haired, fleeting—we don't get
prolonged views of her.

Looks left, looks right.
I feel like I'm searching.
Nicholas always speaks first, hates it.

Searching for what?

Looks left, looks right, looks annoyed.
Don't know. A romance for my narrative.
I could use some sex. Something to feel.

Looks right, looks deceive—

I went home last weekend.
How was that?
I was with my mother and father.
What did you do?
Spent a lot of time in my old room.
How did that feel?
I was bored. Didn't know what to do. I'd read, get up and pace, try to write.
        Just couldn't concentrate.
Sounds like you were anxious.

The session slouches toward sunset.
A flash of pearls, a chartreuse suit.

Last night I had a dream.
Rubs her nose. *Yes.* Pen poised to paper.
I was walking in the yard at my parents' house, the grass was very green, it
        moved in patterns like waves. I felt something strange,
looked down, a small bird
        bright blue, was stuck in my left foot.
Did this scare you?
I tried to get it out but couldn't, tried shaking my foot.
You've had this kind of dream before where something is stuck in you.
The last time it was a cat caught on your hand.

What does it mean?
Her frustration ascends.

If I am the hero of my story,
        then they are the villains.

Get a good look at her
you will want to freeze frame her some day   later

13

she huddles her glasses
her open hands.

INT. MANHATTAN APARTMENT—NIGHT

Nicholas thinks: I fear
what I can't picture,
also what doesn't last.

The mind asleep is key-lit,
passion granting, tasting of
honey & lemons.

I know God loves a good narrative
thick with love, I like to think

He has chosen
a soundtrack.

When I am afraid I won't feel
I think of mundane things I know—
my love of red meat,
my fondness for soundtracks.

INT. PSYCHOANALYST'S OFFICE—DAY

Isabel behind
me, the daybed covered in red

surrounded by pillows. How can you feel
anything but tired
when there is this couch?

What are you feeling now?
Listless.   *Bored.*
Hmm.   *I want to be*

a writer, all I can do is read magazines, jerk off, watch movies on TV.

She laughs, I rage,
want to kill her but fear
prison & confinement,
she relinquishes her tortoise-shell
glasses to her hand.

I have a date tonight.
Really? Why is that surprising?   I hate HER,   I HATE her.
A guy I met at the movies, he's a friend of my friend.

For a writer you don't use many images.
If only I believed in capital punishment, she's my proof.   *Images*
aren't trustworthy.

INT. MANHATTAN BAR—NIGHT

Pavement glistens in the night
putting me in mind
of Film Noir

except this is a date scene, not a crime.

MARK is nice & the streets are calm.

ANGLE ON: silences.

Mark and I
drink two drinks.

He speaks at arm's length
but every word
beckons me to lie

between his echo of arms.

EXT. MANHATTAN BAR—LATER

When I tell him I had fun tonight
he could be my mother,
evasive and sly
like vermouth

he/she huddles over his/her drink,
he/she motions for another,

he/she listens by pretending not to listen,
he/she swirls the olives along the wide rim,
dreaming they will absorb every last drop

olives taste best alcohol-soaked.

INT. MANHATTAN APARTMENT—DAY

Mark and I stand before the door
like statues if statues
wore khaki. A kiss, a good-bye.

I sit at a table, I write, CLOSE UP on notebook,

*There is more drama
in a drop of light than the vast space of your palms*

*you keep too little,
drink too much.*

I want to run away

the circus is dead,
I dream of joining
the movies.

ANGLE ON: a strip of four pictures, each
a wildly different expression.
I paste it
on the same page.

You could be my mother

speak at arm's length
& every word
beckons me to lie

between your shadowed arms.

Part Two: June

INT. MANHATTAN APARTMENT—MIND'S EYE—TWILIGHT

In the beginning was the montage
after this the word, with words

naming starts

like *heartache and inviolable.*

Mark's typical response,   *schadenfreude,*

I make a MONTAGE

FLASH CUT:
       Jagged chest, an inlet, a cove
             covered by Douglas firs.

FLASH CUT:
       Dark features go featureless,
             wind sweeping him clean.

FLASH CUT:
       A prowler's red eyes
             break the dark soup night.

Then, snap of wrist, turn of head, a foot falls. *Wait,*
cause and effect grow unbalanced—

Sirens disrupt,

FLASH CUT:
> I expect explosion, instead…
>> Dawn. Flutter. Night again.

A flourish

the streets, clear and rain-slicked.

INT. MANHATTAN COCKTAIL PARTY—NIGHT

We arrive ten minutes apart because Mark won't arrive together.

What's with all the subterfuge
and toying, I admire more matter, less art, is this love
or a game of chess?

He and I batter our words. Cocktail glasses
bang in the night air.

Honesty is overrated. Why is there no
food at this party?

We're all trying
to get through this journey of living
without giving in to misery and decay.

You sound like a Woody Allen movie, Nicholas.   Can't we
go eat now? There's no
food at this party.

Woody's right
life is divided between the miserable and the horrible.   Hugs kisses
goodbyes exit.

EXT. MANHATTAN SIDEWALK—CONTINUOUS

We walk in fragments of red and tobacco.

To avoid speaking we speak
in quotations—
emotional shorthand for
the jaded.

Where are your charms?

You speak at arm's length,
every word
beckons me to lie.

INT. MANHATTAN APARTMENT—BEDROOM—DAY

Cinema   is death   at 24 frames per second.

What's the difference between life and movies?
No one knows, read Tolstoy but get me some coffee first.

Try not thinking so much.

In the absence of interstitial moments, we

CUT TO:

INT. MANHATTAN APARTMENT—LIVING ROOM—DAY

We're splayed across the room,
blankets on a warm morning. Even our lines mingle.

It's a gorgeous day, come to the beach.   I can't,
I've got to write.   You always do, it's time

you reevaluate your goals.

Everyday pleasures
are inherently

shortsighted

when we are all going to die.   Cinema is death.

Just shut up and fuck me,   write about it once I'm gone.

EXT. THE BEACH—NIGHT

I'm an oyster cuddled with a pesky grain of sand.

I've seen enough movies
to know

how this will end.

INT. MANHATTAN APARTMENT—BEDROOM—LATER

TV screen illuminates
an unmade bed, alone,

two smooth men
fuck on hay,
it smells of bitter almonds and sweat.

I take greedy inventory:
left hand, right nipple,

right hand pushes down my green 2(x)ist underwear
blond hairs decorate his stomach ridges.

My hand imitates

his mouth, I am

hushed, utterly alone.

Only the VCR blinks the hour.

Part Three: July

INT. MANHATTAN APARTMENT—MIND'S EYE—TWILIGHT

The CAMERA focuses on Nicholas's face.

Eyes wide,
in such a room, one can only learn
something about claustrophobia.

Questions screech across his face:

INT. PSYCHOANALYST'S OFFICE—DAY

I can't decide
if I am sad about breaking up or happy about it.

Can't or won't?   (Oh, yes, I hate her)

Silence.

Meanwhile I may go away.   *Where?*
Paris, I can write there.   *It'll be good,*
have a change of scene.   *Nothing bad can happen*
in a city with so many movies screened each day.

Tell me about vacations with your parents—

FLASHBACK TO:

23

INT. SUBURBAN KITCHEN—1978—NIGHT

Nicholas, 8, at the table,
engages pen-and-ink drawing,
aggressive lines jerk across the paper. Mother at the sink,

—Where are we going?
—Florida.   —What's wrong with here? What
will I do there?   —Swim in   the   ocean.
—Are there sharks? —No. —Where do I sleep
in Florida?   —A hotel. —In a bed? —What's wrong with you?
—What will I   eat   in Florida?   —Same things
you eat here,   only I won't have to cook it.

She speaks at arm's length
but with each word
beckons me to lie

between her echo of arms.

BACK TO:

INT. PSYCHOANALYST'S OFFICE—CONTINUOUS

In the absence of Isabel's face,
I focus on hair-line cracks
gray dust webbing across the ceiling.

You didn't feel
safe, wanted to know
you'd feel loved
in Florida. Did I feel loved
at home? You
tell me.

I want to run away,

I dream of joining
the movies.

What's the difference between life and movies?
You tell me.
My goal   never to know.

INT. MIND'S EYE—TWILIGHT

The CAMERA focuses on Nicholas's face.

Eyes wide,
fresh limes.

Questions screech across his face.

What does her face do when I describe my life, what if
images are no more real than tooth decay?

Words cloy
an itch in the middle of my back—

words, words! You've made a rope of words
                    and strangled yourself.

What do words taste like?
Squash your eyes,
picture fresh mint,

soothing scent, her voice sneaks up from behind.

Part Four: August

EXT. PARIS SIDEWALK CAFE—DAY

The cinema knows too much

its love scenes precede mine
what's left is trite.

So what?   A taste of heaven:
It almost made me believe in God.

INT. PARIS APARTMENT—LIVING ROOM—DAY

I lean before an open window,
look left, look right, in hand
Marlboro Light

three weeks in another town.

Rue Vieille du Temple, a fifth floor walk-
up, salmon-colored walls,
a chimney stretches.

Evenings:
I dream of dark coffee.

Paris on celluloid accentuates
the day, ripples
like water on cobblestones.

EXT. HOTEL DE VILLE—LATER

The square is full, people meet on a Friday night.

Your name scribbled on paper
a friend tosses me before I leave

Know anyone in Paris?
Not a soul.

Your face, still blank,

we smile in the rain, light low,
I struggle to say simple things in French.

YOU: 28, Gallic, hair the color of tall wheat—

I forget about my umbrella, nestled somewhere
in my backpack,
your face is key lit, like the Pont Neuf at night.

                                                    DISSOLVE TO:

EXT. QUAI ALONG THE SEINE—NIGHT

Assault of night, a first kiss
the city is magic.

Your face, round,
apples and chocolate cookies.

Pale skin spotted with freckles
you are a road map

I follow home.

INT. LOVE SCENE—NIGHT

What can I say
beyond hyperbole:
lips, mouth, chest, thigh, hand, hips?
All in tight close-up.

After, we lie in bed—

untranslatable
silence: emotion.

A universe of freckles expands

across your shoulder blades.

FADE TO:

INT. PARIS APARTMENT—DAY

Morning light
holds me in its palm.

Smells of bread and coffee:

Come away with me.   *Anywhere.*
Toulouse, like in "Wild Reeds," is only three hours on the TGV. Or to Brit-
tany, like in "Come Undone," which would be closer. We can rent a car.

Though I am heavy with yesterday's red wine
the horizon blinks its red eyes
I race—

beyond the silver rooftops.

INT. / EXT. VARIOUS—DAY

A series of CLOSE-UPS:

His pale hand against a black steering wheel,

Our two faces, seen from right profile, seated in a car, looking in the
same direction,

He in red trunks, me in blue, on the sand-strewn beach,

Running, splashing in the blue-green surf,

He trips me to the sand.

CUT TO:

EXT. BEACH—CONTINUOUS

Walking,
the world, in backdrop
is patient and glad,

hand in hand, a portentous
soundtrack glares,

the CAMERA, bee-like, swirls around us.

INT. BRITTANY HOTEL ROOM—NIGHT

It hurts to look at you. Love is
a horror film:

you pain me, a needle in an eye,
a death deep in my stomach,

you are a mixture,
desire and its opposite.

FLASHBACK TO:

INT. PSYCHOANALYST'S OFFICE—DAY

Everyday pleasures
are inherently
shortsighted
when   we   are   all   going   to   die.

Nicholas lies, behind
Isabel in glasses watches.

No wonder you like film, You're afraid of emotion, Film is life
held at arm's length.
Why would I be afraid of something so everyday?
Intensity's scary, Maybe this is learned behavior from your mother.
You have to say that, you're an analyst.

BACK TO:

INT. BRITTANY HOTEL ROOM—NIGHT

Fighting fear
I focus on

facts: thighs, hips, mouth, back
The scene plays on autopilot:
I happen by your hand.

INT. CAFÉ—DAY

I type at my laptop. CLOSE UP: the screen

I am back from the country, which was moody, cold, gray, and heavy
with rain. The houses are just like the weather but outlined with bright
trying-to-be-happy flowers of pinks, blues, and reds. And everywhere
the barely audible cry of rolling waves and seagulls hovering on wind—
static in the air. We hiked, ate fish, drank red wine. We held hands and
kissed and shocked—a bit—the quiet religious veneers of these quiet
religious old, stone towns of Brittany. He ran along the beach, while I
grabbed some time to write and tried to slow down time and capture it
in any way possible.

INT. PARIS APARTMENT—BEDROOM—NIGHT

A fitful night, Nicholas dreams—

Buildings glow at night from within:
if they were human, you could say
this light was their soul,

the orange of daylight,
the blue of night, the red of the moment
just before you touch me
when everything seems possible, hyper-real, hyperbolic:
played out on a giant, silver screen.

EXT. PARIS PARK—DAY

Floating, a swan of blue
and green fire
eats madeleines by the hour.

I will remember all,
indelible prints.

What is cinema if not a memory? It remembers better than I.

My lips hunger for your smell,
I settle for your touch,
fingers on fingers.

INT. CAFÉ—DAY

I sit at my laptop. CLOSE UP: the screen

We came back last night instead of today. He had this idea last night, before dinner, while walking on the beach to watch the sunset that it would be happier to profit from a full Saturday in Paris together and spend the night driving back than to waste all day Saturday in the car. So, we embraced a French *l'abandon* and checked out of the hotel in a fury and drove til 3 a.m. I am happy to be back in Paris and feel the kind of pleasure upon returning to NYC—back at home and at peace until the tumult of good-byes. I can't decide if this proves that life has some pleasure or if it continues to reveal that life is misery. But I make lots of notes of lines, images, words to use or not to use. The past week has been as good as finishing a poem: I am sure to be overwhelmed with depression from having to say goodbye. I am off to drink coffee and profit from my final days in the city together before I jet to NYC on Tuesday morning—God willing. Hope all is well with you and look forward to exchanging adventures of the past weeks.

INT. BISTRO—NIGHT

We form
a still-life around the table with wine and cheese.

Do you believe in God?
No. Do you?
I'm French.
You're right, God couldn't write such scenes.

Outside, stars flee an orange sky.

EXT. SIDEWALK—DAY

Good-byes pique from under the skin.

I search for someplace genial,
lonesome without you,
streets sink beneath my heavy feet.

My storyline follows its narrative.

The sun hides
behind every obelisk
pinned in the center of each place—
Bastille, Concorde, Vendome—
Perhaps the pointed top will catch a cloud,
a freeze frame, an illusion,

time stops.

EXT. SIDEWALK—LATER

The moon is within arm's reach,

tangible, a lemon
scenting the painted sky,
& God is a movie mogul in a shiny gold tie.

Cinema is   death   at 24   frames   per second.

    I know

       how this story will end

            FADE TO BLACK.

II.

Cinema Vernacular

1.

We open on a mystery,
a riddle has happened, will happen, will happen again

What's the point of experience
if we can't use it?

The scene is New York City, often
turning to look back.
Off set, we learn lines—

Me: friendly and everyday
as a white peach

You: all that I am not,
too beautiful, too young, too glad

My Mom: never bakes, never does laundry,
she is 5'8 and 58

Our Director: fatherly, 65, with thumbs
like God's.

Like a snake a camera lies in wait.

2.

In this scene, our Director explains, *we see
you together for the first time, it is a crowded bar.*

I always look directly into your eyes,
You look primitive, transgressing.

What's up?

Like an actor in a Hitchcock film
your eyes reveal
what your words do not.

Your eyes glaze—
a December pond we'd come across when 12 years old
in Connecticut for a pick-up hockey game—

no wonder they are the color of blue ice.

3.

The scene includes a phone, suggests
distance, you ready?

A brown head nods. Our Director
smiles, hands somersault the air.

What are you up to tonight?

In Connecticut, my Mom lies,
chemicals travel her veins
a tiny train chuffing her off—

it feels like hell, if it works

cheeks sallow, hair fallen,
her body autumnal.

A floppy royal blue hat receives her head.

When I   NEED,
I   get   NOTHING,

I   learn   RESOLVE   instead.

No definite plans. You want to grab a drink?
How about this weekend? I'm off to a party tonight.

4.

A New York street corner, a kiss

You: *You're intense.*
Me: *I'm a poet.*
You: *Wouldn't you sell more*

if you wrote fiction?

5.

The smoke-filled party is in backdrop
the CAMERA holds tight on your faces, your eyes.

Will you be possessive all night?

I am possessive

because I choose to be
I am no longer a ROMANTIC

I won't die without you.
Your slate-colored, cropped hair
goes blond.

The light deceives & the party arrows 2 a.m.

6.

My dream
to go away with you for the weekend
is made

of construction paper, orange
ribbon, & Elmer's glue.

What's the point of experience
if not to use it?

7.

A year ago to the day,
my Mom and I sat for a weekend in Vermont
eating steaks and spring vegetables.

FLASH CUT: an inn, evergreens—

She said *Let's come back next year,*
ignoring the groan forming in her breast.

8.

Your skin, luminous, a naked penis, a pale head.

9.

A street corner, a kiss goodnight

You: *You're intense.*

Your palm grazes my head.
I walk away

often turning to look back.

10.

My bed is a failure.

It flaps about like a fish, while you and I lie
motionless, hushed

letting the world do the work.

It smells of stale, pink peonies.
A camera hums to the right.

My mouth fills with ideas of your skin.

In the blue dark, our fingers connect
then walk apart.

On My Father's Watch

the trees grow incidental
the sky lurches

and the day's nucleus explodes rain.

Everything saturates. It's late July. But—
weren't we *thirsty* for it?

It makes me think of *Genesis.* No, not *Genesis* but of Dickens—
his ability to create whole worlds, microcosms so effortless,
the marks aren't visible when he carves life from paper.

After, how the light makes everything yellowed, an old photograph.

There was a time—*wasn't there*—
when desire taught something
other than patience?

I want you
your Omega watch tells a lie

time is a bad joke.
Every day is Tuesday at 12:32. Tuesday. Tuesday. Tuesday.   *Isn't it?*

No wit or drama can change what is.

Can't you and I have a conversation

on a bench by the sea wall under
the green-screen sky, picking up a thing or two
about how to live apart?

Behind us, old oaks must be nine
stories high, more vertical
than nature would seem to allow.

Suite, Summer

INT. MANHATTAN LIVING ROOM—TWILIGHT

As OPENING TITLES roll
a voice-over: *rise to wake me from some sharper daydream.*

I didn't have a body until you

narrow legs, an awkward frame

running alongside you
the beach smells of blue heat, our bodies
travel in rhythm.

If I were Shakespeare, the time I waste before time
wastes me,
I'd pun madly about you.

Instead I waste my will
on expensive vodka
and title my autobiography:

"Incredible Adventures in Mirrors, Doppelgangers, and Truth-Tellers."

Because you can't *will*
someone to love,

                                    even the leaves blush, say no.

INT. FIRE ISLAND BEDROOM—DAYBREAK

Lean, bend, part

a lanky reed by bay's edge is threatening to shatter
by evening, wind won't carry us anymore—

we...

        consider turtles:

a breezy attitude
one envies so much,
if they were suspicious, they'd have breastplates.

They're perfectly independent
with homes of knucklebone.

EXT. FIRE ISLAND POOL—LATER

This isn't about the foods you won't eat,
it's about your eyes
the color of coriander.

If I were medieval I'd down them
as a restorative medicine,

along red and orange pine trees
two evanescent Jews, up a Chagall canvas

Spanish moss cries between us
tickling like the small, coriander-green hairs of the beach's dune.

                SLOW DISSOLVE TO:

EXT. FIRE ISLAND DECK—TWILIGHT

A shock of lightning

DISENGAGES

sky from ocean.

SLOW DISSOLVE TO:

INT. MANHATTAN LIVING ROOM—DAY

We replace touch with voice
though the cradled phone can never be
your fingers on my neck.

Outside my window boys get their hair cut,
emerging glad and pretty,
a new landscape.

FADE OUT.

Sanctuary

I tell him I won't betray loose thoughts.
I tell him I want to swing
from rafters, like breath.

I tell him I'm in love.

My father's face like Notre Dame's
is watched by gargoyles.

Behind rose windows, he searches
day-darkened stones
read as liturgy,
hanging with candle soot and confessional's sweat,
carved in like wrinkles.

I ask him to unlock heavy doors.
I ask him to embrace me like ringing bells,
grant me clemency,
this shakes his rock rigid brow,

turns his foundations to wine.

And So, And So

He's made of repetitions and digressions

however, when I see him
I don't speak.

His walk is a stutter

and so, and so, he goes

going but sometimes not,
                              he stops—

so then we talk some but when we talk
we also feel: mercurial

then it's time to nap, eat something
                                        chocolate.

And so, and so, he goes

going but sometimes stopped, he's not

and so then we talk some, but when we talk
we also taste, or rather, feel

and so, and so, like two lanky bodies trapped in a long glass tube
heating up. And so, and so.

Building Grandfathers

The buildings in Paris are grandfathers, lying in beds of stone, rough and gray from years of steak and wine. They want to tell stories about their youths, if only anyone would listen, days of sun beating down on rock façade, carving wrinkles in walls that are traceable like history, stories of hand-in-hand strolls down tree-lined walkways in parks well-manicured by geometricians, who can plot trees by precise, algebraic formulations. Memories become words as easily as breathing out hot smoke from a cigar. Grandfathers do not move and are more like pictures in the museums, keeping us guessing with false syllogisms. Through long arterial galleries that run through the Louvre, I look for ghosts from the heady days before electricity in vaulted walls, gilded wood beams, higher than any tree.

Memoriam

When you died, I was seven,
another broken toy.
Now, I pine to know you,
my mouth, bitter with a salty jealousy
of those who did.
I remember the explorer,
      foraging the nearby forest for insight: our prey?
      hoping to avoid the encroaching wild.
I remember the alchemist, transforming
      water sugar and string
      into rock candy:

I remember my adoration of the magician.

I ask my father about you—
      the chemist trapped in a business suit—
but his words are in an unknown language
long dead.
Melting clocks drip their tears through
a strainer, unsatisfying memory.
I climb
the mountain to find your small, flat
black-and-white portrait, touching
only weighty wind, blowing me down.

Images are actually
      fish, pulling them out of the water,
they flap about and suffocate: unattainable
like the foxes, deep in earthen burrows,
you and I hunted with walking sticks as our guides.

My legacy from you,
a dictionary inscribed with
your name and office floor
up top the city, watchful among the clouds.

Begin: Ode to Beginnings

As if I were a tree wind whispers   *baby*

He's at my leaves   *strangely*   wild desert violets in New England
          I am out-of-place   (or he is?)   He is too gentle for a hard frame
and the echo of gin on his breath   hangs in the air like music,

he   in me   IS   melody:

meaning *a parade of notes, one following the other meaningfully:*

a melody is a series of linear events or a succession, not a simultaneity as in
a chord. However, this succession must contain change of some kind and be
perceived as a single entity (possibly gestalt) to be called a melody. Most spe-
cifically this includes patterns of changing pitches and durations, while most
generally it includes any interacting patterns of changing events or qualities.

He in me is mechanical. That's not to say
anything critical, rather being E X A C T and when he walks
there's mechanical pressure, strong wind.

He in me is a late blooming flower, built
of delays, he extends smiles
meaning…the absence of meaning

beginnings are blooming orange daisies.

Long teeth, sunken eyes
small creases spring from them, lines
around a yellow ball in a child's drawing.

As if I were a TREE   wind in my ear whispering *baby*.

Begin: Ode to beginnings: they are colored   ORANGE!

Red Snapper

lies beneath branches of thyme—
I pebble it with coarse salt and pepper.

Even in death he smiles like a saint.

On the carpeted floor, we're
ancient Romans, our legs
curl in a knot I can break
free of. Drops of wine
splash my arm. I effort
to please, tell him I've made it
before. *(I have watched,*
but watching isn't the same as doing.)

Even in death. Smiling like a saint.

Pink flesh flakes onto a hungry fork.
He eats, goal-oriented.
The fish is delicate, easily it will break,
shoulder touching shoulder,
nothing left but skeleton.

III.

STANZAS

1.

Three days   after my
Bar   Mitzvah,   I re-
call clearly   reading
a   new   disease, world-
wide   Bergen Belsen
I   would be   just as
fated   to   acquire
because   who   I was
growing   up   to be.
Now   a man   but for
how   long could I hope
to last   here   living,
a world   sick with me?
What   of the   rabbis
whowatchedme forhours
of   study,   fortified
me   to   stand   before
a   large crowd speaking
words learned in rhythm
who   could   turn away
as   I   prayed   to the
ripemuscled   brightboys.

2.

While   my feet   dangle
off her crimson couch
my   grandmother
tells   me   stories,
her   hands,   a hand-
kerchief   folded
calm   on   her   lap,
the Vienna music house
where   she   walks up
and   down   aisles
to   see   the   clothes
European   women
wear,   she,
twirling   white beads
against   her   neck
stones chafe skin red.
One day   she and my
father   walk   in,
me   in   mom's   dress
weight   of   fabric
draping   me   like
Jesus   over   Mary in
the   Pieta.
I vanish   like   skin
beneath   blue   silk.

3.

Last week,   my mother and father
came   into   New York   for dinner
she   holding   *The Jewish Ledger*
BEING JEWISHANDGAY read the
cover,   as I shuddered not sure
which I found more embarrassing.
I wince   at   mental images
boys   hovering   over me,   bent
over,   us shaking   in rhythm
davening   to me,   their torah
I   am   flesh   in   the   religion
while old men in beards turn away
can't she see they think I leveled
Babel's tower—,   the word in me
resounds like Kiddush without wine.

4.

In Russia,   soldiers stole
from   Jewish   villages
boys, who   hid themselves
in fields,   closets,   cellars
anywhere   opaque.
A face   reveals   too much.
You learn to blend with dirt,
I   hid   among   folds in
air,   labored   to stay quiet,
not like morning   glories
shining   leaves as sun dawns
down   each   morning
but   like a worm   who digs
through feet of rich dark
coffee   grounds,   tastes
warm air,   then tunnels   on.

5.

I   had   an   excess
the   summer   she died
second   grandparent
in nine weeks, quick as
red   hair bleeds   white.
A   summer of deaths
comes   too   easily.
Part   of   me
bled out when   the boy
emerged   from behind
darkened,   heavy rocks
free, no more ties, raise
high the damned shroud
off   me,   I've   risen.

6.

In this year   of quiet living
theserooms, ourhome, becomemysong
bare, boxed, white walls my melody.
When first we met   and fell in love
we learned to fight,   learned to hug
Passion   floods,   next day trickles.
These days our work drowns the night,
down to bed,   not even   a kiss.
Awake   to   museums,   movies
distractions   to fill   eyes like lights
on menorahs blind for eight days.
Where   are soft kisses   full as songs
composed   lives spent together?
For   the years   of quiet   living
we   haven't finished   our journey
back to that place   where first we met
steadily   back,   to our first date
I,   an old fisherman,   rowing

Fog

It's three o'clock,
our train from Rotterdam folds into it.

I have never seen one that didn't lift.

Cyclists in orange appear,
then vaporize.

Fog bleaches everything.

We enter fog like time,
hesitant,

as if remembering someone near the mind—

I *was* a fog,
fumbling from boys to girls to boys.

(You, Doctor, remind me
the flip side of fear is wish.)

The sky slackens from silver,
though before
it was dense as cotton,
mercury-

gray, strands caught and hung in branches.

Things I Am Not Sorry

I didn't know we couldn't speak about the time
I lost my mouth.

I am not sorry I wore your negligee the color
of lemons, I am not sorry
I composed dances to your capricious
hairstyles, I am not sorry your breath
was flakes of wind.

You arranged me like furniture:
here, my fingers to smile,
here, my eyes to hold the truth, here
my nipples to keep the moment.

You arranged me to kiss,
but I ironed over the crease
where my lips lived.

*I am the guy who disbelieves
wisdom is in better hands.*

What compels you
to smash me, foot first,
beneath my window?

My hands are tie-dyed
a touch-patch garden of golden rod & violets
& my body falls across the bed
like so much clippings of auburn hair.

Portrait in Blues and Greens

You talk most
when you are hungry. There is a HUNGER

for misunderstanding
found in conversation.

I see you in shades of blue and green.
Like the northern lights—*aurora borealis*—you reach
over the frozen blue-green sky, the shade of arctic sea.

The irregular
way light punctures a chlorine pool
like white noise your hard stomach surrounds me.

You see me in shades of meandering
deception,
patch of black ice, frost heave

what you call a gentle rain, I call a torrent.

Your every blue word is green with a hundred thousand questions, doused
amid the acrid smell of last week,   like chlorine,
I cannot lose that scent,   nor help but include you in my dreams

when you lie   so perfectly lavender   with sage in counterpoint.

HOME MOVIES (2 WEEKS, 4 REELS)

Reel 1:
Cartography, After 6 Months

The bathroom faucet is a metronome,
it clocks and wastes the delayed day,
the boundless anticipation of a hotel room.

Visiting you is like seeing Israel,
a second home,
a bold blink of a monarch's wing.
If I were smarter, I'd chart
every minutia—your face drawn leaner,
pale skin, defiant against sun
glowing like night air in winter.

In minutes we'll enter an airport embrace—
you'll become holy, the dusting of freckles
across your nose, shimmer turns of eyes,
beatific scraps to entomb in an old city's hill.

Reel 2:
Blood Oranges

Driving, we compare our analysts,
it's play with Barbie dolls, we hold
them up, show a hairstyle, a new-fangled
outfit no one had considered.

Suddenly a kibbutz appears—in groves
hundreds of tiny suns hang on green
as stars pasted in sky.

Wild trees along the highway
are landscaped, embrace all opposites,

where blood exclamations remain
an étoile, color the land magic,
irrigating even oranges' veins.

Jerusalem ripens everything,
everything is beyond history.

Reel 3:
Jerusalem Song

(after Sylvia Plath)

These are the mind's construction stones—
built, as if reliquary themselves.

Cold, blessed.

I compare them to teeth,
infused in cigar, bold-boned,
dyed-in-wool, coffee teeth.

They could be my grandfather's—
row upon row
climbing along the Old City's wall.

If I were historical I'd come armed
with scrub brushes and Lysol.

Instead these stones are transitional
wind between their crevices
imitates music.

Reel 4:
In the Laundromat

Sassy Spanish girls fold & flirt
staccato teeth & air
their world's the corner of Prince Street
even here, especially here, I long for
those Israeli soldiers
fresh wild olives
young as my students
I teach them poetic
conviction
they expect meter
walk about
taut as sheets
infinite imperium
redux Abraham & Child.

Hollywood, Windowless

The oven in the kitchen heats more
than my bedroom. The windowed room, seems windowless,

heavy like Hollywood Boulevard roaring below. Give me

a window, he prays, but gets Hollywood instead.
Windowless, there are no prayers for this, only dreams

the way honeysuckle cries out
the way light unravels

inevitable, aching
claustrophobic as a rubber mask—

Hollywood's a window and Hollywood's
windowless, even in white daylight everything appears

like this darkened. How can this place be so windowless when
forecasts are for laurels to fall? Drowning

is melodramatic, as are screams over Hollywood

& I'm in a moment both breathing and choking
like so many. Outside wind flakes in curls of tarragon and garlic,

snagging in someone's grayed hair, banking,
windowless, beneath your too luxuriant pool.

Poem (Movies Predict)

Lana Turner   (gets up)

leaves Kirk Douglas's house

walks out of   THE BAD AND THE BEAUTIFUL

to fling herself   like a white dress,
         flung into her car,
     Lana turns it out: *betrayal, humiliation*—

        sudden, like rain

                deluges the windshield.

It's true. Movies predict us—

             *   *   *

Like Bette Davis

when you become red-hot,   like the way Bette Davis

    shoves *words*

    at Gary Merrill in   ALL ABOUT EVE

Davis downs her drink, hands the glass to Merrill,
leaves,   CAMERA   with her.

Lana Turner   *lives*   the DVD like cinema is death

as CLOSING CREDITS roll
she curls between us… smoke from a tongue…

                                        CUT TO:

…gray glazed cobble stones, the Meatpacking District yawns—
                    a crescendo of smoking sun,

and I'm Bette, I'm Lana, everyone edged   blonde & dirty

a long night dancing
behind us, the city is

like the boy in A STREETCAR NAMED DESIRE, innocent & perverse,

a spider's netting
electrifying dark danger

figuring you: the integral X Y,

as a jazz score   syncopates
sloe gin riffs

                            like DESIRE,

and blues raining: horns, horns, horns.

Everything is musical score: *tongue, hair, & ripple*

Flick a cigarette to your shoe. You and I know *liaisons* are dangerous.

It's true. These movies

        are over-referenced

                which makes me love them.

Fugue for an Affair

I.

Your smile hovered
above me like the sun, following me.
It was such a surprise I found myself looking
from odd places: cars, bed, random shuttered windows—
happy to see the sun still there.

A miracle had taken place,
the long winter blossoming,
you transformed my desire.

II.

Your words
blossom and burn—
Faulkner never imposes,
mint julep images slide
on ice, he had the patience
of a Southerner.

III.

You said

You have a heart of amber
a fly trapped in its middle.

IV.

I ripple and sway under you,
collapse like a suspension bridge

sending us, me, you
into cold blue.

V.

On the couch we're conjoined
with the Sunday Times.

What will we have for breakfast?
More coffee.
What after that?
Toast and eggs.
Who will make them?
The one who didn't make the coffee.

VI.

Your fingers
on the small of my back

reinvent touch.

I've said too much. Because I need,
you retreat—

Your back arches, falls.
A candle flickers
on a bedside table.

VII.

You said

You have a heart of amber
a fly trapped in its middle,

I see now
this was projection.

VIII.

Your hand
a bull's-eye,

your tongue
an algebraic code.

IX.

Games to play
in place of sex:

spy, love, war—

my thoughts, like the palm of night,
turn vermilion.

X.

In the future
I will try a less-is-more
conversational style:

for example x
for example y

for example,
the same thing

happened to me.

XI.

You said

whoever returns will write about this.
If you return

there will be a murder.

XII.

Street lamps replace
the moon, cobblestones look
green. To pass the evening
we eat shrimp and drink vodka.

From the roof of the night I foresee:

I will not go along
I will not put up with anything
I will pack my pen, my shoes, my dandelions
and I will flee these city stones
on horseback or wings.

You will search for fingerprints,
find shadows.

NOTES

In "These Months," "Cinema is death at 24 frames per second" is my memory of a phrase from a paper given by Laura Mulvey at the Alfred Hitchcock Centennial Celebration Conference at New York University in October 1999.

In "These Months, Part III," I quote Norma Desmond's line "Words, words! You've made a rope of words" from Billy Wilder's *Sunset Boulevard*.

The definition of "melody" that appears in italics in "Begin: Ode to Beginnings" comes from Google definitions.

"Poem (Movies Predict)" is inspired by Frank O'Hara's *Poem (Lana Turner has collapsed!)*.

ACKNOWLEDGMENTS

Grateful acknowledgment is made to the following journals and their editors: *Arc/angel* "Memoriam"; *Barrow Street* "Suite, Summer" and "Begin: Ode to Beginnings"; *The Paris Review* "Cinema Vernacular"; *Response* "Stanza 1," "Stanza 3," and "Building Grandfathers"; *Marsh Hawk Review* "Jerusalem Song"; *Shampoo* "Screenpoem #2" (excerpt from "These Months"), "Things I Am Not Sorry," "Reel #4: In the Laundromat," "Hollywood, Windowless," and "And So, And So"; *Slope* "Fugue for an Affair" and "These Months" (part four); *Third Coast* "Screenpoem" [excerpt from "These Months" (part two)].

My tremendous gratitude to the generous teachers, colleagues, and mentors who showed me what poems are and how to make them: Frank Bidart, Harold Bloom, Tom Fink, Allen Grossman, Yusef Komunyakaa, Gretchen Mattox, Martha Rhodes, and Sharon Olds. Thank you to Patricia No, Antonia Pinter and everyone at Publication Studio. I'd also like to thank my friends and family for their love and support: Michael Silverman, Bill Handley, Gail Appell Nickowitz, and Allyson, Dan, Luka, and Hazel Ross. And my love and gratitude to my dearest friends and beacons in writing, who read and gave invaluable advice and encouragement on these poems: Deborah Landau, Bill Oliver, and Ron Palmer.

ABOUT THE AUTHOR

Peter Nickowitz grew up in Fairfield, Connecticut and graduated from Brandeis University and New York University, where he received a Ph.D. in English and American literature. His poems have appeared in literary magazines including *The Paris Review*, *Barrow Street*, *Shampoo*, *Slope*, *Marsh Hawk Review*, and *Third Coast*, and he was a National Poetry Series finalist.

He is the author of *Rhetoric and Sexuality: The Poetry of Hart Crane, Elizabeth Bishop, and James Merrill* (Palgrave, 2006). His plays include *The Alice Complex, Backgammon at the Louvre, Songs & Statues,* and *Love, Alters, Everything* and have been produced at the Cherry Lane Theatre, Dixon Place, The Blank Theatre, and Stella Adler Studio, where he was the 2008-09 Harold Clurman Playwright-in-Residence. He has taught at the City University of New York, the University of Southern California, and the New School, and currently teaches in the Liberal Studies Program and the Goldberg Department of Dramatic Writing at New York University.